I'm Not Feeling Well Today

by **Shirley Neitzel**

pictures by
Nancy Winslow Parker

Greenwillow Books
An Imprint of HarperCollins Publishers

The artist wishes to thank Cascade Toy
for permission to reproduce their hand
and finger puppets throughout this book.

The stained glass window on pages 31
and 32 is copied from one in the Loveland
House, circa 1867, administered by the
Bay Head (NJ) Historical Society.

I'm Not Feeling Well Today
Text copyright © 2001 by Shirley Neitzel
Illustrations copyright © 2001
by Nancy Winslow Parker
All rights reserved. Printed in Hong Kong
by South China Printing Company (1988) Ltd.

Watercolor paints, pencils, and a black
pen were used for the full-color art.
The text type is Seagull.

Library of Congress
Cataloging-in-Publication Data

Neitzel, Shirley.
I'm not feeling well today / by Shirley Neitzel;
pictures by Nancy Winslow Parker.
    p.   cm.
"Greenwillow Books."
Summary: In cumulative verses using rebuses,
a young boy describes all the things he will
need since he is not feeling well—until he learns
that school is closed because of a snowstorm.
ISBN 0-688-17380-2 (trade)
ISBN 0-688-17381-0 (lib. bdg.)
1. Rebuses. [1. Sick—Fiction. 2. Stories in rhyme.
3. Rebuses.] I. Parker, Nancy Winslow, ill. II. Title.
PZ8.3.N34 Ik 2001   [E]—dc21   00-021917

10 9 8 7 6 5 4 3 2 1
First Edition

I'm not feeling well today.

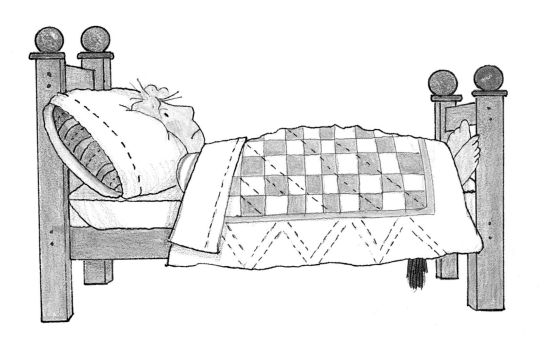

I need a box of tissues, in case I sneeze,

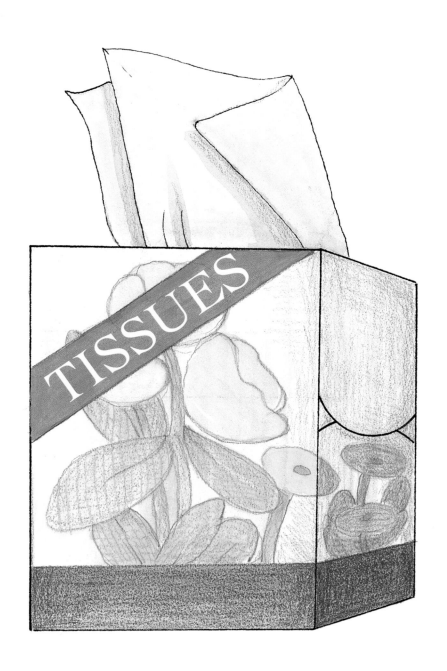

since I'm not feeling well today.

I need an extra blanket, if you please,

and a in case I sneeze,

since I'm not feeling well today.

I need another pillow for my head,

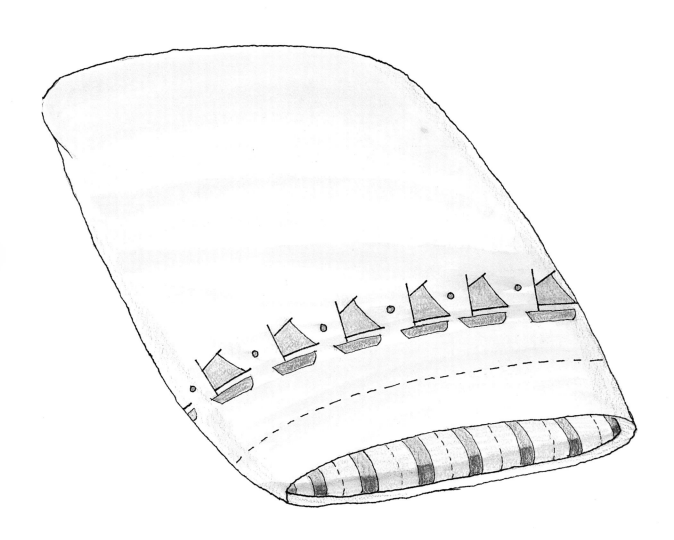

and an extra  if you please,

and a  in case I sneeze,

since I'm not feeling well today.

I need Clyde the cat with me in bed,

and another  for my head,

and an extra  if you please,

and a in case I sneeze,

since I'm not feeling well today.

I need all my puppets for a play,

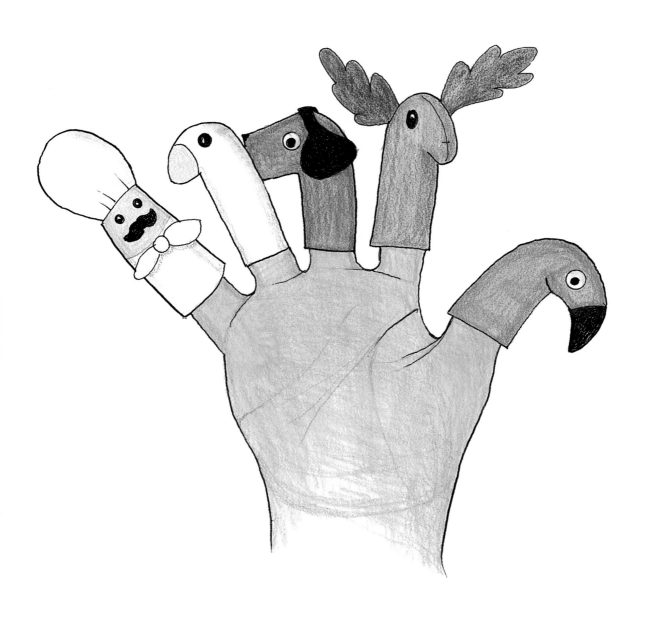

and Clyde the with me in bed,

and another for my head,

and an extra 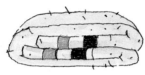 if you please,

and a in case I sneeze,

since I'm not feeling well today.

I need jigsaw puzzles on a tray,

and all my for a play,

and Clyde the with me in bed,

and another for my head,

and an extra 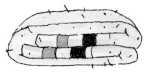 if you please,

and a in case I sneeze,

since I'm not feeling well today.

I need cartoon programs on TV,

and 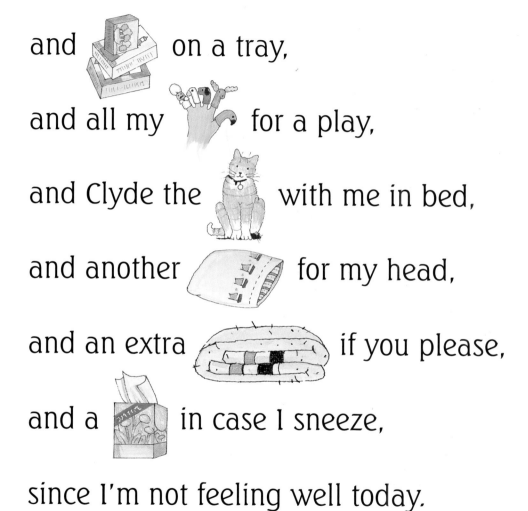 on a tray,

and all my for a play,

and Clyde the with me in bed,

and another for my head,

and an extra if you please,

and a in case I sneeze,

since I'm not feeling well today.

I need cinnamon toast and lemon tea,

and 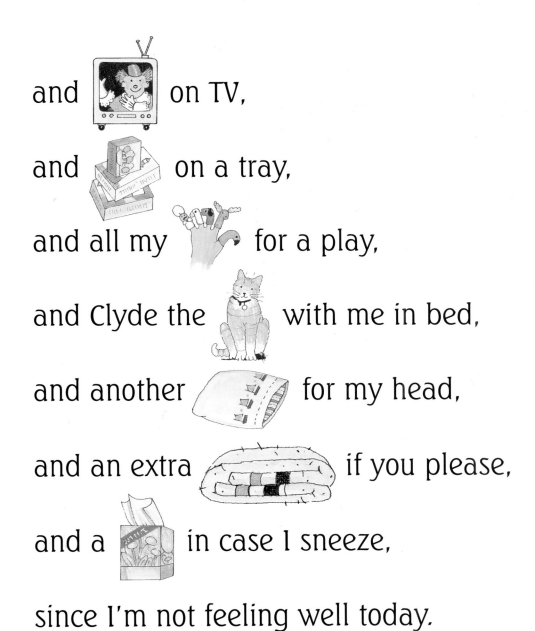 on TV,

and on a tray,

and all my for a play,

and Clyde the with me in bed,

and another for my head,

and an extra if you please,

and a in case I sneeze,

since I'm not feeling well today.

I need my bear, my special friend,

and 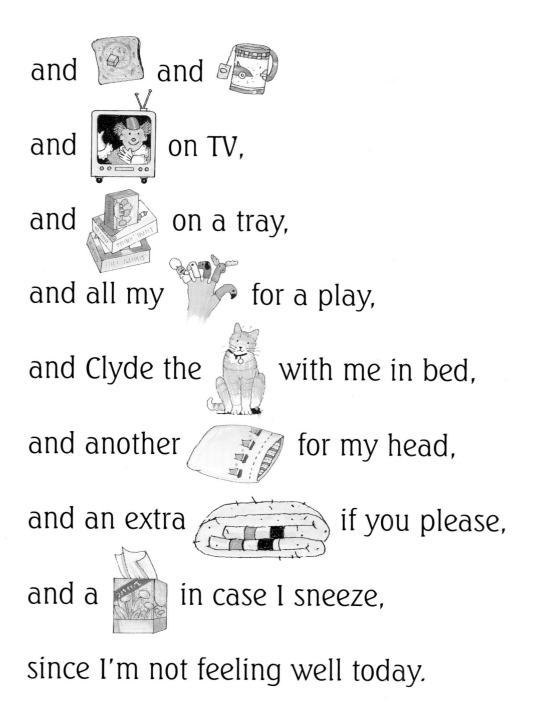 and

and on TV,

and on a tray,

and all my for a play,

and Clyde the with me in bed,

and another for my head,

and an extra if you please,

and a in case I sneeze,

since I'm not feeling well today.

Please read this book from front to end

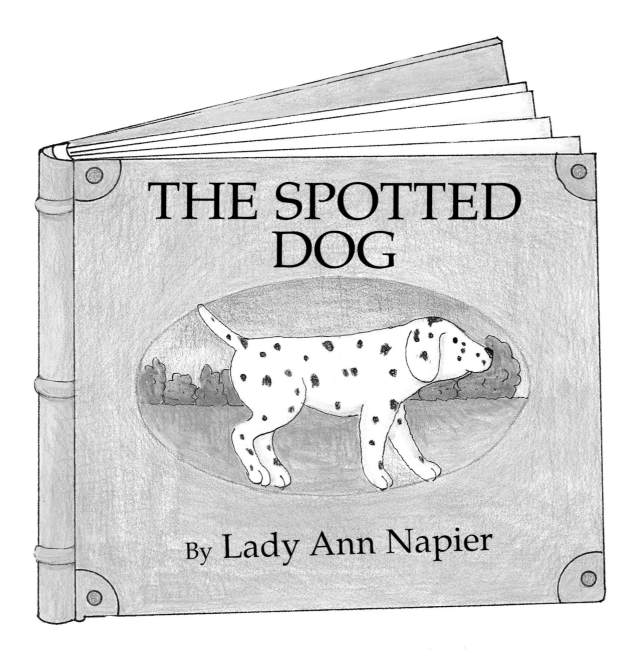

THE SPOTTED DOG

By Lady Ann Napier

to me—and  my special friend.

We'll have and

and watch just you and me.

We'll build on a tray,

and use my  for a play,

while Clyde the sleeps on my bed

on the fluffy for my head

under the  snug as you please.

Pass the  in case I sneeze,

since I'm not feeling well today.

What's that?

You think I'm not so sick
because I did a tumbling trick?

You say if I were really ill,
I'd not complain, I'd just lie still?

I wouldn't ask for all my toys,
or jump, or make a lot of noise,

or carry on, or raise a fuss?

Is it too late to catch the bus?

The school is closed? I cannot go?

The storm last night left too much snow?

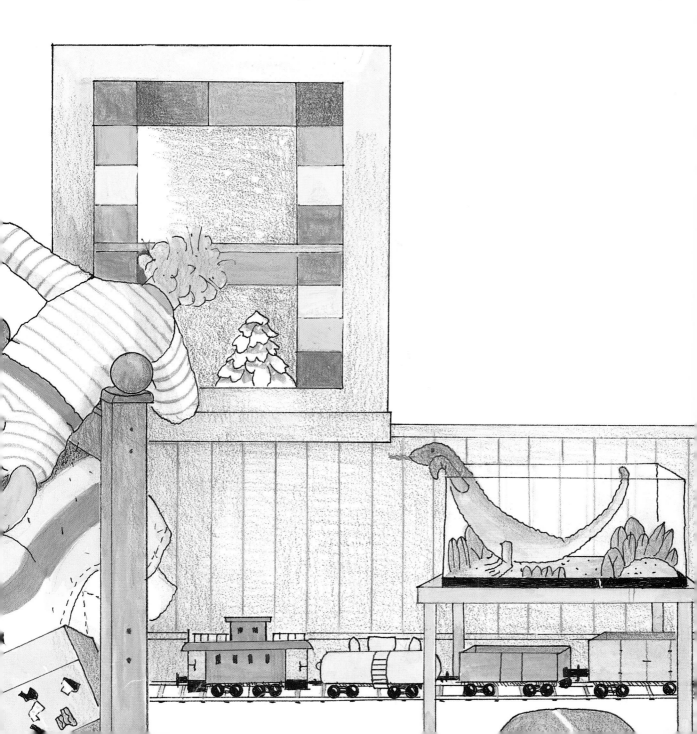

That is too bad! Hurrah! Hurray!
I'm glad I'm feeling well today!